THE ART OF NATHAN SAWAYA

Forward
by Scott Jones

It's hard not to look at Nathan Sawaya's sculptures and privately think, "Hey, I could do that."

Or, "My six-year-old is also a really awesome LEGO builder. Maybe he can have a museum show some day."

Or, "You know, I myself built some pretty terrific things out of LEGO in my day."

Or, "What's all the hoo-hah about? So what if some weird crackpot built some things out of LEGO? Who cares?"

Don't be embarrassed. It's natural to think these things. It's perfectly OK.

LEGO is usually found in toy stores. And the only contact most parents/adults have with LEGO is when they step on a stray brick in the middle of the night. But if you're looking at Sawaya's pieces while thinking one or all of the above thoughts, then you're not seeing things clearly. You're going to have to put your nostalgia aside. And put your LEGO bias aside. You're going to have to open your mind a little and try to see beyond the LEGO bricks.

After all, you don't look at Roy Lichenstein's work and think, "Nice comics." You don't look at something by Warhol and say, "That reminds me, I need to pick up a few cans of minestrone on the way home." Look at the architecture in Sawaya's pieces. Look at the craft involved. Look at the intricate brick work. Look at how Sawaya has managed to create organic-looking sculptures that defy and celebrate the very medium they're created in at the same time.

Sawaya is a surrealist mash-up of forms and artists. Imagine Frank Lloyd Wright crossed with Ray Harryhausen, or Auguste Rodin crossed with Shigeru Miyamoto, and you start to get a sense of where Sawaya is coming from.

Because of the nature of the medium, you're likely going to want to touch Sawaya's sculptures. (I strongly advise not doing so, unless you'd like your day at the museum to be cut short.) Why? Call it the gravitas of LEGO.

It's nearly impossible to look at something created out of LEGO and not want to start building yourself. It's almost as if your fingers remember what it's like to hold those plastic bricks in your hand. Close your eyes for a second, and you can practically hear the sound of two bricks fitting together with that almost primordial LEGO snap. There's something immensely comforting in that snap. It's the sound of everything fitting together perfectly. Taking things a step further, it's the sound of the world making sense for one, brief moment.

Beyond setting aside your own memories and LEGO bias, get yourself a bucket of LEGO bricks. Sink your hands into the bucket. Snap a few bricks together. (Trust me, it's better than any anti-depressant.)

Only then will you truly appreciate the magnificent works you are about to see.

Scott Jones is a writer based in New York City.

"A lot of my work suggests a figure in transition. It represents the metamorphoses I am experiencing in my own life. My pieces grow out of my fears and accomplishments, as a lawyer and as an artist, as a boy and as a man."

~Nathan Sawaya

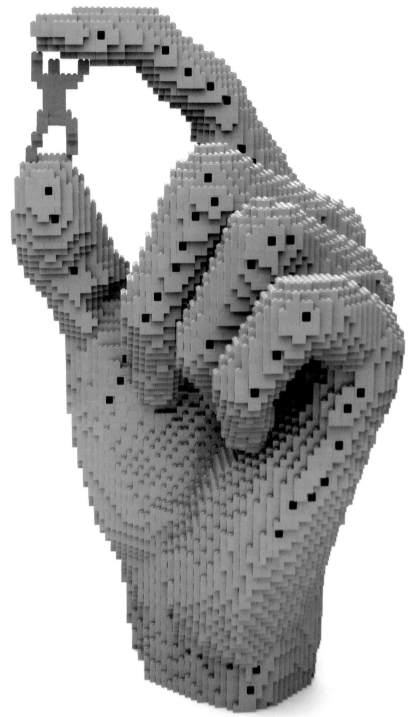

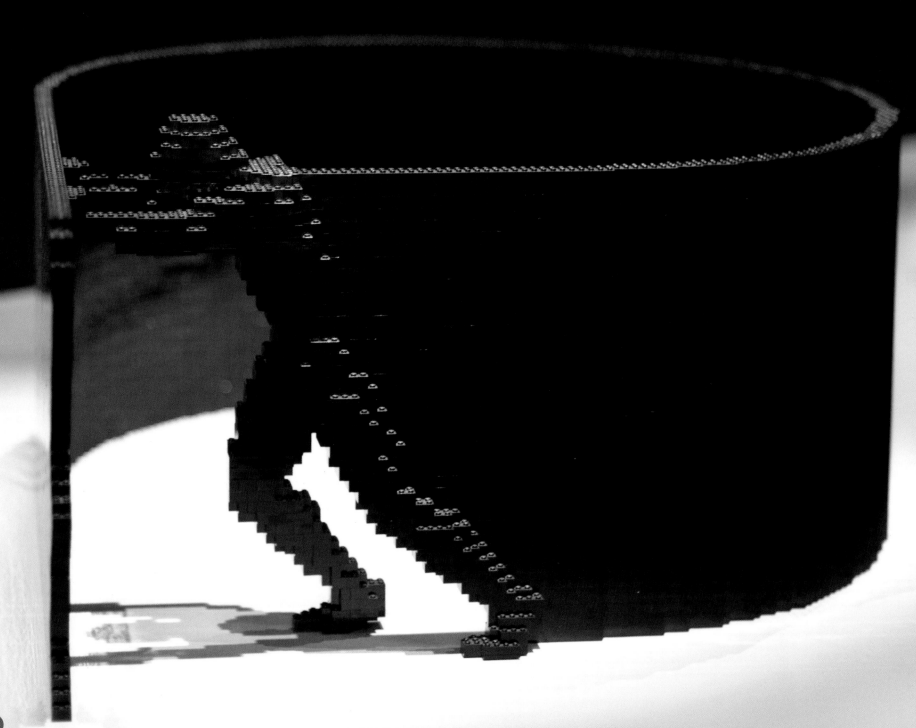

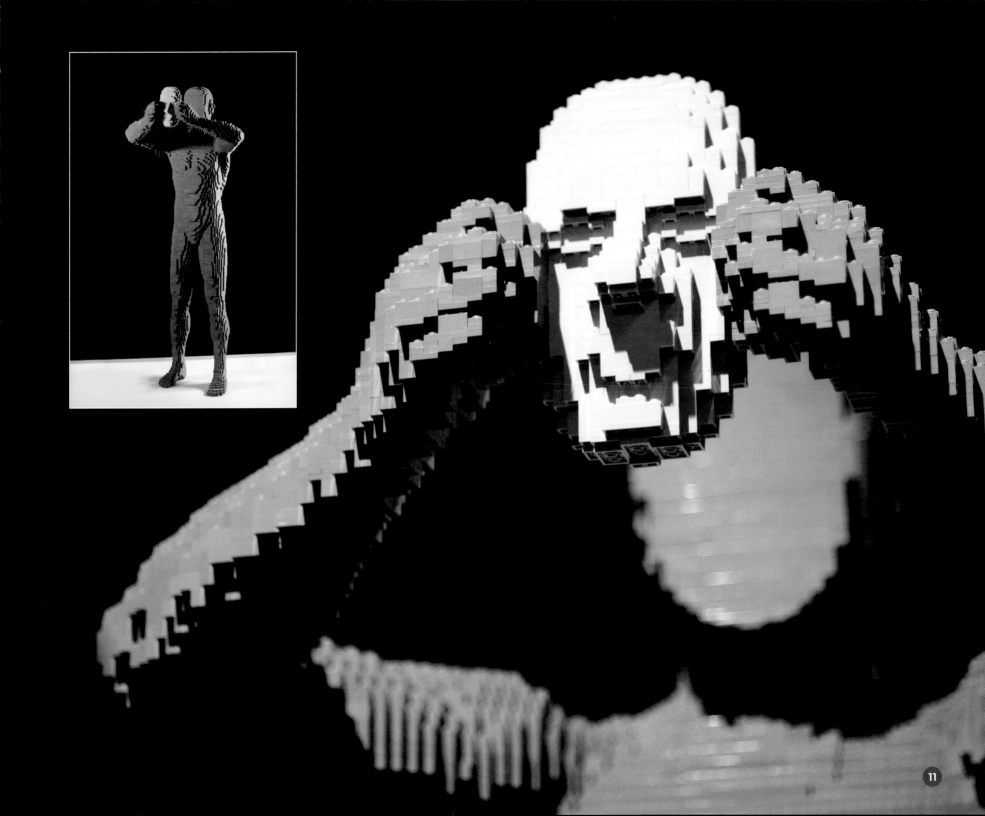

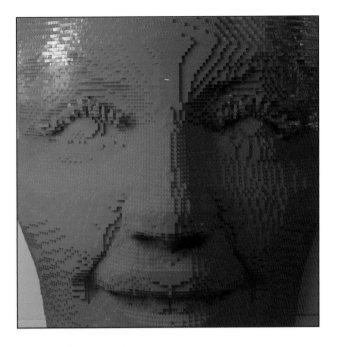
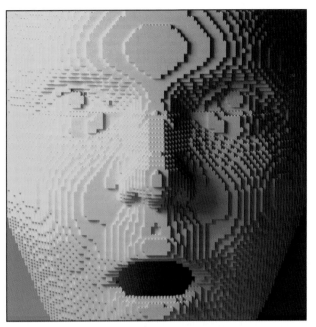

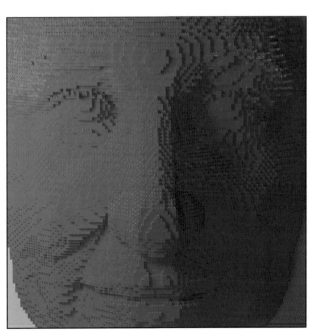

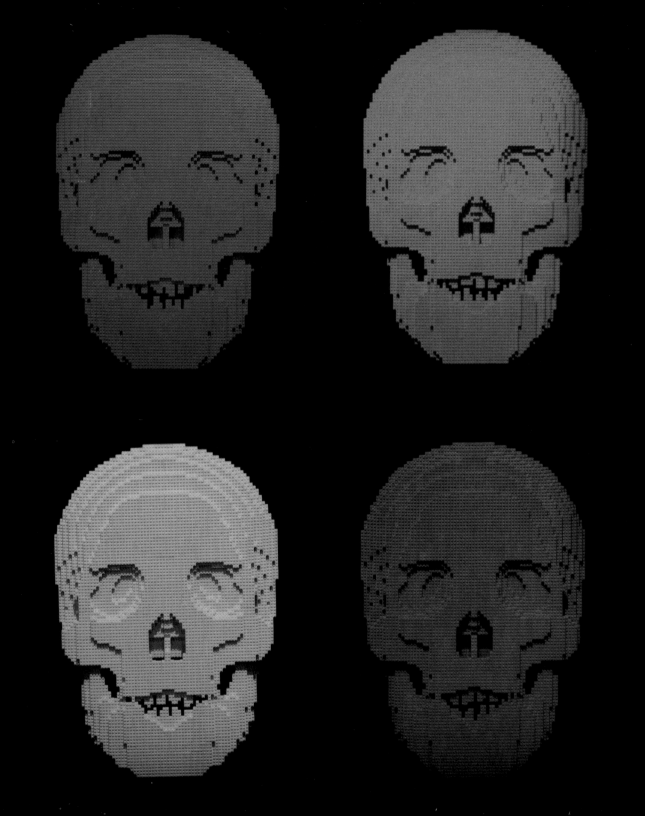

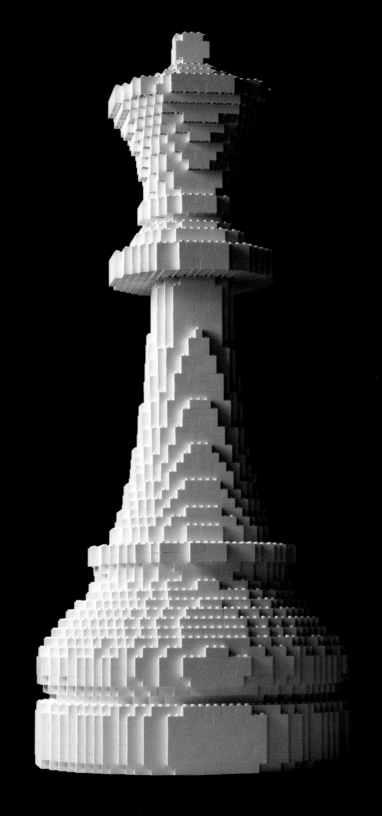

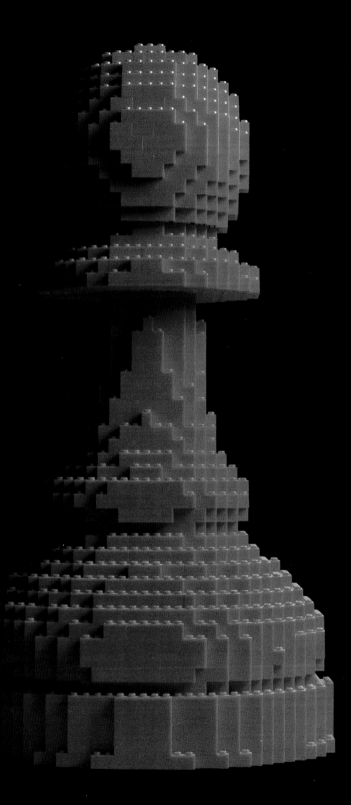

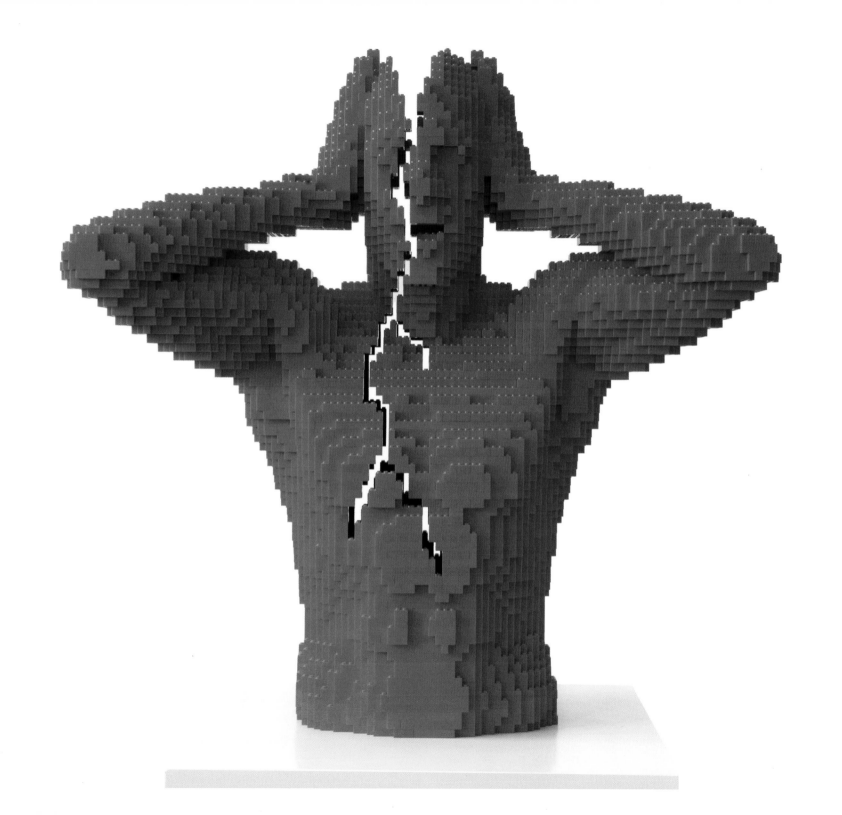

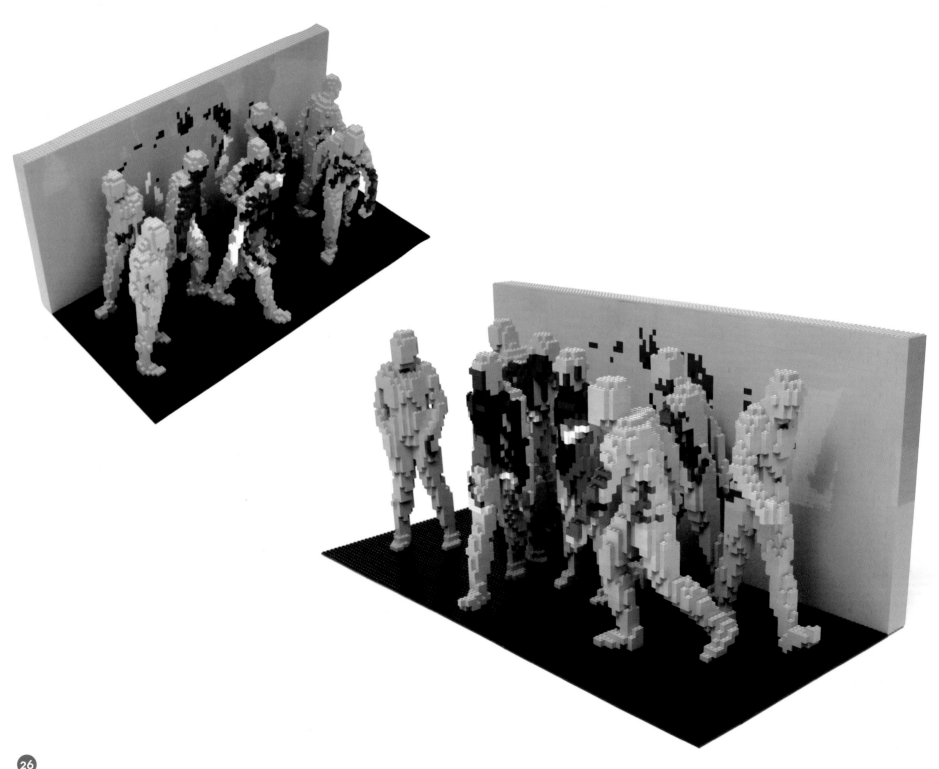

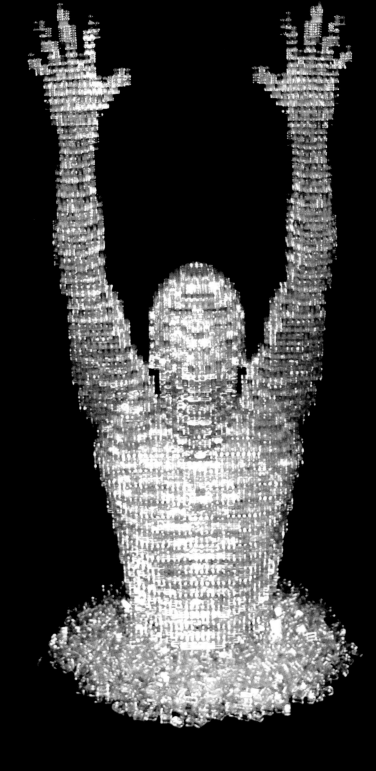

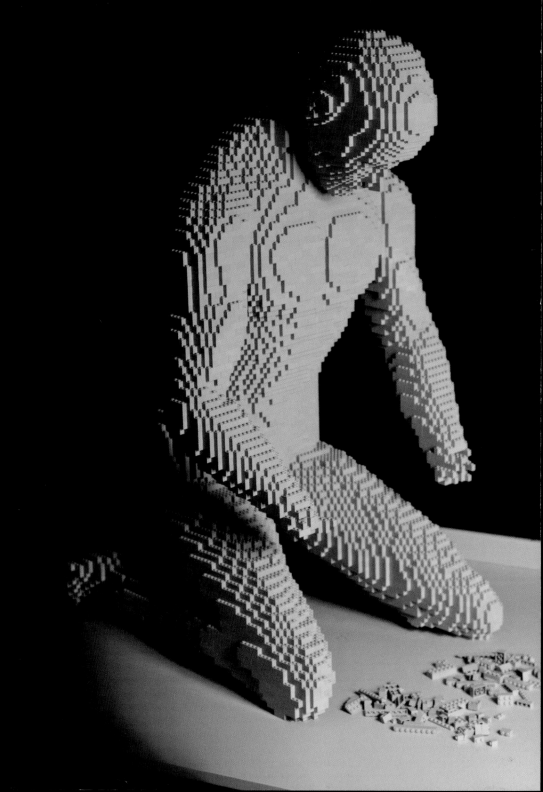

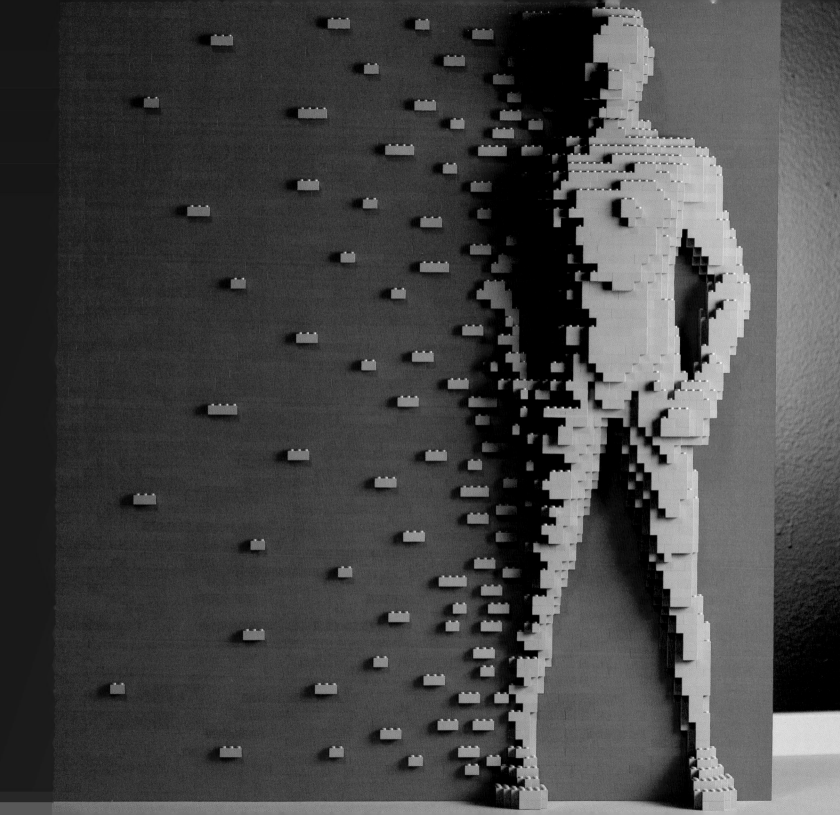

"Hugman likes to give hugs. He hugs sign poles. He hugs park benches. He hugs bike racks. He hugs fence posts. He hugs almost anything he can fit his arms around. Hugmen can be found from New York City to Australia and other places in between. They are my version of street art – LEGO graffiti if you will. They show up where I am, and tend to stay for a day or two before they walk off. Kind of like me."

~Nathan Sawaya

Directory

5

Blue Sky
32" x 39" x 17"

Blue
34" x 42" x 18"

6

Red
49" x 24" x 26"

7

Everlasting
42" x 34" x 12"

Strength of Spirit
38" x 21" x 21"

8

Gray
45" x 45" x 13"

9

Black White
45" x 15" x 11"

The Writer
27" x 18" x 8"

10

Untitled
42" x 42" x 15"

11

Mask
71" x 29" x 24"

12

Untitled
20" x 40" x 12"

13

Red FaceMask
45" x 42" x 20"

Yellow FaceMask
38" x 32" x 16"

Blue FaceMask
48" x 40" x 18"

Untitled
20" x 40" x 12"

14

Yellow
28" x 35" x 19"

15

Skulls
74" x 54" x 3"

16

Courtney White
45" x 45"

17

Untitled
32" x 32"

18

Stairway
38" x 40" x 15"

19

Peace by Pieces
30" x 30" x 4"

Untitled
57" x 19" x 13"

20

Queen
32" x 14" x 14"

21

Pawn
20" x 10" x 10"

22

Swimmer
30" x 13" x 79"

23

Cracking Up
32" x 33" x 15"

24

The Courage Within
59" x 18" x 11"

Kiss
27" x 21" x 20"

25

My Boy
41" x 38" x 24"

26 - 27

Crowd
18" x 17" x 37"

28

Melting Man
38" x 16" x 16"

29

Green
70" x 27" x 15"

30

Despair
32" x 28" x 17"

Hands
39" x 22" x 25"

31

Disintegration
35" 32" x 6"

32

Rebirth of New Orleans
66" x 42" x 64"

33

Hand
54" x 31" x 37"

Pointing
83" x 23" x 19"

34

Hugman
16" x 5" x 6"

35

Hugman
16" x 5" x 6"